Birthday Tributes

To those you love,
tell them why, tell them now

Joy Pritchard O'Donnell Dawn Pritchard Burruel

Birthday Tributes

Visit our website at **www.birthdaytributes.com**

Cover artwork and family tree illustration by Bryan Burruel

An Amethyst Moon Book
Published by AMETHYST MOON PUBLISHING
P.O. Box 87885
Tucson, AZ 85754
www.ampubbooks.com
ISBN 978-1-935354-62-8 / 1-935354-62-0

First Edition 2011

Library of Congress Control Number: 2011916804

This memoir is comprised of the authors' recollections and impressions of the actual events as they occurred in their lives. In the interest of privacy, some names have been omitted and some timelines have been compressed.

Birthday Tributes

*To those you love,
tell them why, tell them now*

Joy Pritchard O'Donnell

Dawn Pritchard Burruel

Contents

Grandma
Grandpa
Dad
Mom
Joy
Bonnie
Dawn
Michael
Jesse
Bryan
Molly
Juliet

Part One

~

The Introduction

Birthday Tributes: The Idea

Joy

My birthday was approaching. My family had always made each person's birthday a special day. We celebrated, as many families do, with the birthday person's favorite food for dinner, a cake with candles, making a birthday wish, everyone singing "Happy Birthday," and presents to open.

This year, my family had fallen on hard times financially. The country was in a recession. Jobs were hard to come by or non-existent. Several people in my family were out of work and struggling to pay bills for the necessities of life. I knew that I didn't want anyone to spend money on presents this year.

Over the years, it had oftentimes struck me as odd that people would tell someone what he or she meant to them, put words to the qualities they valued in that person, after the person had died. I didn't want that to happen in my family. We'd been through a lot together, the ups and downs of life, as have many families. I wanted us to acknowledge what we loved about each other, what we meant to each other, now.

And so, I told my sister, Dawn, that I didn't want any presents that cost money for my birthday. What I wanted, I said, was a "Birthday Tribute" from my family. I wanted them to make my day special by sharing their memories of me and telling me what I meant to them. Dawn took on the challenge and became the organizer and writer of the first Birthday Tribute.

It turned out to be the best birthday gift I have ever received.

Birthday Tribute

♫ Joy ♪

Mom named you Joy because it was her best friend's name, and it had a beautiful meaning. Mom and Dad knew they had chosen the right name for you, because you brought so much joy to their lives.

When Mom was in labor waiting for you to be born, she kept asking what time it was. She wanted you to be born on November eleventh, so that you would get to celebrate your birthday on a holiday.

Mom's best friend was so pleased that you were named after her, that Mom believes their friendship deepened and lasted because of it.

Dad loved your name so much he said it twice, "Joy, Joy." To Molly, you are her "Ju-Ju," and her "Joie."

The first to be born, your Grandparents were mesmerized by everything you did. They were sure you were the most brilliant child ever (turns out, you were).

As a Daughter, Granddaughter, Sister, Sister-in-Law, Aunt, Great- Aunt and Teacher, and a wonderful person, you have led the way with: honor, caring, strength, wisdom, kindness, encouragement, compassion, warmth, dedication, generosity, thoughtfulness, the patience of Gandhi, and the love of Mother Teresa.

We admire you for the things you have done: becoming and sticking to being a vegetarian, following your political principles, traveling the world, setting your educational and career goals high, and always achieving and exceeding your own expectations.

You have overcome the tough parts of life, and somehow you always seem to rebound stronger, better and even younger than before. Your strength in character, dedication to life balance and pursuing your love of music is an inspiration to us all. You are, and will continue to be, the change you wish to see in the world.

We turn to you for: guidance, motivation, answers to trivia questions, help with homework, someone to listen, organization, spell check, help in emergencies, advice, music and

Joy. ♫ ♪ ♫

Birthday Tributes: The Challenge

Dawn

As far back as I can remember, I had always worked (even before I was supposed to). The summer when I was 13, on a dare from a friend, I applied for a job as a car hop on roller skates at a drive-in restaurant a few miles from my house. I was hired. Then I had to find a way to get to and from my job. I walked or ran, depending on how late it was. But I always went, no matter what.

I earned enough money to buy new clothes for school. For the first time in my life, I would have something new to wear that I bought myself. I would have something that wasn't a hand-me-down from one of my sisters or a neighbor who had girls older than us. Because I had earned the money myself, I was allowed to spend it on what was important to me. At age 13, clothes, makeup, and how I looked were definitely important to me. At that age, I remember deciding whether it would be a good day or a bad day based on what I had to wear.

This was when I began to develop my Minnesota work ethic. From then on, I always worked. I would pour myself into whatever the job was and, in some cases, almost allow the job to consume me. At one point, I heard the phrase, “If you love what you do, you will never work a day in your life.” I soon realized what I loved to do was to work.

Suddenly, during a time the country was in an economic recession, I found myself unemployed and feeling disconnected from my profession. I had reached the end of my financial rope. My sister Joy’s birthday was approaching, and I was worried about getting her a gift. Then, one day, she asked me to write a Birthday Tribute for her as a gift. She made it clear that she didn’t want anyone to spend money on gifts this year.

Joy had spent the past year walking along side of me, as we do whether times are good or bad. As the younger sister, I owed her so much. When she told me what she wanted was a Birthday Tribute, I knew it was what she *really* wanted. The one thing it would require from me was the one thing I never used to have but did have now—time.

I hoped to give her the best tribute that anyone would ever have. I thought about who should be involved in the process and what information needed to be gathered. I wanted the tribute to reflect the whole person, past, present, and future. I have to admit I drew my first inspiration from her name—obvious, right? Her name certainly made it easy to find Christmas gifts for her for many years. Joy is certainly what she brings to us. So, it made sense to begin and end with her name. I set out interviewing the members of our family, starting with our mother, asking them what they loved about Joy.

What followed was a month of discussions with the members of our family. I took a walk down memory lane with each person. I tried to note the aspects that signified the best of her. I asked similar questions of myself; my husband, Michael; our sister, Bonnie; my sons, Jesse and Bryan; my daughter, Molly; and my granddaughter, Juliet. While what I heard were sometimes similar aspects of her, everyone also had something new and wonderful to add. We were acknowledging and sharing what she brings to our lives, what we admire about her, and what she means to us.

On Joy's birthday, as we gathered for the cake and song, I read her tribute to her aloud. As I read the words that captured the essence of this person who means so much to me, it was hard to get through it without crying. I realized during the reading of her tribute that what we had created was a true celebration. It was a gift to us all.

I knew then that a tribute from my family was what I wanted for my next birthday.

Birthday Tribute

Dawn

Daughter, Sister, Wife, Mom, and Grandma. To us, your family, you are nurturing, caring, kind, loving, creative, compassionate, and loyal.

As a **Daughter**: You've grown from being a companion to Mom on her Avon route to being her helpful, loving caregiver in her senior years. You loved mashed potatoes as a child and became the family gourmet mashed potato cook as an adult. You always tried to reach out to find the love in Dad, and he appreciated that in you (even when he didn't know how to show it).

As a **Sister**: You share our childhood memories and our grown-up dreams. As the youngest, you "followed directions" and "played well with others." You followed directions to skate down the icy hill to the Keewaydin hollow. Now as an adult, you have become a leader. There is no better friend than a Sister. And there is no better Sister than you.

As a **Wife, Mom, and Grandma**: You have given us the best gift of all in the children we cherish. You are the best "TwiMom" on Team Edward. The best "TwirlMom" in the baton world. The best 2nd mom (and future mother-in-law) in the world. You rock on the Beatle's Rock Band game, and you always make delicious food for everyone to enjoy. You have a smile to make a thousand angels sing. You are the best pancake maker in the world.

We all depend on you to be our family cook, hair stylist, faithful friend and our rock.

You always make sure that our holidays and family gatherings are special times.

You make us glad that "we are family."

Part Two

~

Our Stories

From Cold to Hot

Joy

In May 1975, I moved from my hometown of Minneapolis, Minnesota, to Tucson, Arizona. At the time, I didn't know it would be a permanent move. I didn't know I was taking a pioneer sort of role for my family. I didn't know of the events that, over the next year, would mean that my sister, Dawn, and my mom would follow me. All I knew was I couldn't go through another Minnesota winter. It was an attempt to thaw out.

A few days after Christmas 1974, my friend Merry and I left Minneapolis for a trip to Mexico. We were two girls in our early twenties bored with the winter and eager for an adventure in the sun. Traveling in Merry's Ford Maverick, we drove from Minneapolis to Texas, then down the east coast of Mexico and south to Oaxaca. We spent a few glorious months in Oaxaca, immersing ourselves in the culture, going to the zocalo everyday, meeting people, taking photographs, exploring the ancient ruins of the Zapotec and Mixtec cultures, and basking in the sun and sea of as yet undiscovered beaches.

When we left Oaxaca, we drove north to Mexico City and then up the west coast of Mexico. In March, we crossed the border at Nogales, Sonora, back into the United States. As we were driving up the highway to Tucson, Arizona, we turned on the car radio and heard our music for the first time in months. Having always been a car-singer, I started singing along to the songs on the radio. And then, Merry joined in. We sang along with Johnny Nash about our bright, sun-shiny days. Music has such a way of evoking moments and memories. Every time I hear that song, I remember those carefree, optimistic days and my journey with Merry.

Merry's boyfriend was spending the winter in Tucson, as did many of our Minneapolis friends trying to escape the winter. He had a comfy little adobe house in a barrio neighborhood. I stayed with them for a few weeks until Dawn and my mom, also eager to have a winter break, drove down from Minneapolis (in my mom's Ford Maverick) to pick me up for a return drive. Fords were big in the middle-class mid-America of the 1970s.

It was April when we returned to Minneapolis, and there was still snow and ice on the ground. It seemed to me the Minnesota winters of my youth lasted from October to June. The bone-chilling cold, the blizzards, the heavy snow that needed shoveling, the icy sidewalks, and the skies that could be heavy with low-hanging clouds all went on way too long. I was always cold and depressed during those winter months. I craved warmth and light.

Those who loved winter, like my high-school boyfriend,

tried to get me to see the "good" side of winter. In tenth grade, he said, "Stick with me baby, and I'll show you the winter of your life."

Well, I did have a great time with him. He was my first love. The winter cold outside meant we spent most of our time inside. We did a lot of hanging out with our friends, in each other's basement rec rooms. We listened to our music, songs from the Beatles, the Stones, and all of the wonderful new sounds of the British Invasion. We went as a couple to school dances. We did all of the latest dances, and best of all—we slow danced. But, the winter never got better for me. I still hated it.

My grandma's family had moved from Holland to Canada before immigrating to the United States. I once asked her, "Why did your family choose to move from Canada to Minneapolis?" She said it was because her mother had wanted to move somewhere warmer.

I tried hard to stifle my laughter and said in a questioning tone, "And she chose Minneapolis?"

I guess, compared to the frozen tundra of Canada, Minneapolis had seemed quite balmy to my great-grandmother. The need to find a warmer place was in my genes. Maybe I went overboard. Tucson isn't just *warmer*. Tucson can be hot as hell for several months of the year.

My niece, Molly, recently asked me, "Joy, when you decided to move to Tucson, had you been to San Diego?"

And so it goes.

A New Life

Dawn

Growing up in Minnesota, I never felt lucky that my birthday was in January, for obvious reasons. The typical ice-skating party, which was planned for winter birthdays, would almost always fail due to weather that even die-hard Minnesotans couldn't handle.

But for Christmas in 1975 and as an early birthday gift, Joy sent me an airline ticket to visit her in Tucson. I missed her desperately, and even the Minneapolis neighborhood where I lived, called Uptown, wasn't much fun in the winter. I didn't want Joy to be without family for Christmas. So, in December, I boarded a plane and headed for the sun, my sister, and her new life. I felt lucky this time. This year my birthday was going to be different. The gift of this trip was the beginning.

My sister was living with her Tucson Guy (a new love in her life). They were happy and comfortable, and they made me feel the same way. We hit many of the sightseeing spots in

Tucson. I saw my first bighorn sheep and rattlesnakes—yikes—at the Arizona-Sonora Desert Museum. I walked through streets reminiscent of the old west at Old Tucson Studios. We hiked among the majestic saguaro cacti in Sabino Canyon. I felt the awe-inspiring beauty in the old church at the San Xavier Mission. The desert and its dwellers were so different from what I knew. Beautiful pastel colors had replaced the black and white movie of the Minnesota winter I had been living in.

They took me to their favorite eateries. Their favorite vegetarian cafe with the grass roof and outside patio became my favorite, too. It was great to be able to eat outside in the winter. Wherever we went it seemed you could order Mexican food, really good Mexican food. I was being introduced to flavors I had never tasted before. In the 1970s, spicy food was hard to find in Minnesota. I was beginning to fall in love with Tucson. When we sat at Gates Pass, watching one of the most beautiful sunsets I had ever seen, I knew I had to come back.

Sitting in the warm sun working on my tan, I began to feel the same ease and comfort as my sister felt. No one in Minnesota believed you had been on a vacation unless you came back tan. So, getting a tan was a top priority. It felt like time had stopped, or at least slowed down, while I was there. I felt safe. Safe was a new feeling. Safe was good.

I was, however, the person who would be considered the least likely to ever leave Minneapolis. It was home. Home was everything. I was grounded in Minnesota. I loved the seasonal changes and all the traditions (and hassles) that happened every few months. I knew and understood the sense of ending and renewal. Minnesotans' conversations usually begin and end with the weather in some way. I was one of them.

I flew home from my trip on New Year's Eve. To celebrate, the flight attendants handed out gift baskets with cheese, fruit, and wine in little bottles. As we approached my beautiful city, the pilot turned off the cabin lights so we could see the city lights. I saved my gift basket. I thought that I would celebrate with my roommates and friends when I got home. After all, it *was* New Year's Eve!

As I climbed the six flights of stairs to the top floor of the old Victorian mansion where we lived, I listened. I didn't hear the traditional noise that usually came from our floor of the house. Most of the time, I would hear the stereo, or one of my roommates playing her guitar, or laughter coming from the kitchen. This time there was no sound. No one was home.

They had forgotten I was coming home that evening and had gone out without me. I had never walked into this place alone. I felt more alone at that moment than I ever had before. Something changed for me that night. The comfort was gone, and the familiar feeling I had known was not the same. They all came home soon after. They realized they had forgotten I was coming home that night, and all was well. But, I felt different. Somehow, I knew things were about to change for me. I just had no idea how much, or for how long.

I was beginning to realize I needed to do something, but I didn't know what that would be. The party of my youth was ending, and a new season was beginning for me. By summer, I discovered I was going to be a mother.

Joy came back for her first summer visit since her move to Tucson. We had our traditional Minneapolis sister time. We went downtown for lunch at our favorite Japanese restaurant and shopped at the elegant Dayton's department store. There in the ladies' lounge at Dayton's, I told her I was pregnant. I was worried she would be angry with me, or maybe disappointed. But, she wasn't. Instead, she calmly asked me what I wanted to do.

I told her I wasn't sure about the logistics, but that I was really excited about becoming a mother. Although I know she was worried about me, I think she was excited, too.

She asked me if I wanted to come to Tucson. She said I could stay with her until I figured it all out.

I knew I had to tell our mom next. I was surprised when she reacted the same way. She was happy, too. I couldn't help but wonder how I would do this without her. I couldn't imagine it. I needed her now more than I ever had before. Mom was also at a transitional point in her life. Since my sisters and I had all moved out, she had sold our house in south Minneapolis. Now she was trying to create a new life for herself. She was searching for what would make her happy and feel fulfilled.

Our mom was a farm girl from a small Minnesota town called Sacred Heart. During World War II, she moved with her family to the Oregon coast to work in the war effort. After the war, they came back to Minnesota and settled in the big city of Minneapolis. By then, she was a pretty, young woman.

She was easily swept off of her feet by a charmer like our dad. When she met him, they were both working at Dayton's.

They married young and started a family. She hadn't planned for it to fall apart. She had wanted the fairy tale. Unfortunately, she hadn't picked the right prince.

She spent her best years putting her daughters first. We were grown now, and she was free to discover what she wanted for herself, with no ties. Fortunately for me, my soon-to-be-born baby, and ultimately for all of us, what she wanted *was* ties.

She didn't hesitate when I told her I wanted to move to Arizona to start a new life. She said, "I'm right behind you."

Unlike many people who move to Arizona, I did not leave Minnesota solely because of the weather. I thought I was grounded in Minneapolis. I had come to realize I had to leave in order to grow. I was not going to find myself in that progressive, wonderful, cosmopolitan city. So, on a hot summer day in Minneapolis, I did leave. I left with forty-seven dollars in my pocket and a baby growing in my belly. I went to discover what hot really meant in the summer and to start my new life with my family in the Arizona sun.

Birthday Tribute

Mom

M is for the love of **Music** that you shared with us.

• We were proud as children to watch you sing with the Keewaydin Mother Singers.

• You introduced us to some of the world's greatest singers: Tony Bennett, Doris Day, John Gary, Rosemary Clooney, and more.

• You made Christmas special, singing carols with Johnny Mathis.

• You provided us with musical instruments and lessons, even though you had to take apart the stairway to get the piano into the basement.

O is for your **Open mind** and love of all people.

• You taught us, by example, not to judge people by appearance, ethnicity, personal issues, or economic status.

• We have watched you gather many diverse, unique, and eclectic people into a group of friends, whom you always enjoy.

• You always find a way to share what little you have with others showing that giving is what is important (and that it can be done with very little money).

• You lend a listening ear and stand steadfast with those who need you.

• You hold true to your beliefs and demonstrate in practice the American principals of equality and acceptance for all.

T is for **Teaching** us how to be crafty.

• We cherish the Christmas ornaments we made as a family and still have today.

• You always made sure that we had a beautiful Christmas tree, even when you had to chop one down in the front yard and bring it in.

• You achieved your goal in art and education through obtaining your college degree and by sharing your artistic gift with others.

• Although we may have teased you for saving everything, you are the person we all come to when we need that piece of ribbon, a tool, or an item that no one else can find.

H is for the **House** that you made a **Home**.

• You chose the perfect neighborhood, complete with lakes and falls. You gave us "a good place to be from."

• You allowed us to fill the house with pets, making them an important part of our family.

• You taught us, through example, that girls can use tools and fix things.

• You showed us that making a home can include: planting a garden, painting a family apple tree on the kitchen wall, and building a patio or even an ice skating rink.

E is for **Everything** you've done for us and making sure we had **Enough.**

• You clipped coupons and ordered groceries so that we always had enough to eat.

• You taught us how to sew and sewed for us, so that we would have clothes to wear.

• You gave us freedom to grow so that we would become independent and strong.

• You taught us about our Norwegian heritage and traditions.

R is for the **Rest of the love** you have to give, and for:

• The reality you always told us to question.

• Always being with us and teaching us about what really matters.

• Making fish sticks and macaroni and cheese.

• Always making me feel welcome, and for always having chocolate.

• • • • • •

I spent the next months preparing for the birth of my child, as most expectant mothers do. Mom had followed me to Arizona, and together we set up a nursery with some of the things she had saved from when my sisters and I were babies. Some were things she had sewn, and some we had sewn together. Beautiful blankets and a multitude of little dresses from the 1950s (made from fabric you couldn't even get anymore) filled the room in anticipation. We washed them all by hand, pressed the ones that needed it, and hung them on little hangers.

I had made a new friend in Arizona. She was from Minnesota too, and was the younger sister of one of Joy's friends. My new friend knew I hadn't met many people in Tucson yet, and that I needed help, so she threw a surprise baby shower for me, inviting all of *her* friends. They all came and filled the needs of the nursery. It was one of the many incredibly thoughtful and selfless things I would begin to experience with the birth of this child of mine.

I was so grateful to have this new life coming my way. I knew this baby and I deserved a fresh start. Having so few friends around was a difficult change for me. I had spent the last few years living in a crowd of friends, being carefree with lots of distractions.

I was beginning to discover just how strong my family was, and that our commitment to each other was unwavering. I wanted Joy to be there with me in the delivery room. She has always been so calming in nature and a levelheaded decision maker. As the hours passed and they finally wheeled me into the delivery room, I looked up to see my sister walking in wearing all of the hospital-required surgical garb. Under the paper shoe covers, she was wearing the traditional Tucson flip-flop sandals. The sandal in the paper shoe cover thing wasn't working at all. She could hardly walk. I burst out laughing and the two of us laughed until *he* was born. Suddenly, after all of the waiting and anticipation, I had a son in my arms. We both continued to laugh and cry while we fell in love with this new life we would call Jesse.

Due to complications, we had to stay in the hospital for seven days. During that week, I had to learn to use my voice in many ways to speak up for myself and my little son. It was the beginning of a new me at the same time. I learned that week becoming a parent is like walking through a door you can never go back through. I would forever be a mom.

When I got home and saw the nursery, the dresses had come down and blue had been added to the room. Thank goodness for mothers.

My days were filled with awe at this new life. Having grown up in an all-female household, I think it was a special gift that my family was given a boy. Some testosterone to balance things out a little was a good thing.

I would spend the next years devoted to being the best mom I could be. I was learning how to love and care for someone who loved me back, unconditionally.

When I had first learned I was going to be a mother, I had no idea just how strongly this child would bond my family back together. Through Jesse, my family rediscovered a sense of celebration that seemed to have been lost for some time. My sisters and I had been going through the struggles of learning to become independent young adults, and in doing so we had been going our separate ways. What we had before us were beautiful holidays filled with joy and happy times, while watching our boy grow. Watching him, we rediscovered our youthful ability to play. He filled our lives with purpose and direction.

Each day, I found new ways to move forward with a new career, new friends, and a new man in my life. This new man was hard working, honest, caring, and he asked me out on a date. I realized at that moment I had never been asked out on a date before, officially. I said, "Yes," and we had a terrific time together.

He was wonderful with my son and as our relationship grew, he bought a house and asked us to move in with him. We were young and in love, and trying hard to mesh who we were with what we wanted in life. What we had was very new for me. We discussed things and made decisions together. I felt for the first time I had and deserved the love and respect of a man. What a different world, sharing a bathroom with a man, sharing a life with a man.

Most of our challenges seemed to revolve around the kitchen. He was a hunter. He had grown up hunting with his dad. He loved it, and he wasn't going to stop just because I had an issue with a dead rattlesnake in our freezer. He was who he was, and he stood up for it. I respected that.

By then I was in the beauty business, and a hairdresser

always works on Saturdays. He would find things he and Jesse could do together. One Saturday before I left for work, he asked me for ideas, as he was fresh out.

I said, "Why don't you make cookies?" So the two of them, my man and my little son, both clueless on how to attempt this major feat, set out to make chocolate chip cookies.

He only called me once, to ask me where the recipe was. I told him it was on the back of the chocolate chip package. At some point, they decided it might be easier to make one big cookie.

He thought it was too hot a day to turn on the oven. So, being an avid camper, he lit the fire on the gas burner, got out the frying pan, and plopped all of the dough into the pan. I came home to two very bewildered guys looking at what resembled vomit in my best pan. We laughed until we cried.

He showed me an Arizona I had not seen before by taking me to places I had not yet been. We camped at Roosevelt Lake with his friends. Twenty years later these friends would come to my door to pick up their daughter Pilar who, ten years later, would become engaged to marry my middle son, Bryan. When I got homesick for Minnesota, he took me up to Mount Lemmon to visit the snow.

We both tried hard to make it work and to build a life together. But, we discovered that some things are so deeply a part of you that they are impossible to change. When he came home one December evening to find a lit Christmas tree in his living room window, he knew this would not work for him.

He had been raised by his father under strong Jewish

traditions and beliefs. He valued those traditions and beliefs, and he wanted to continue them with his own family. He tried to involve me in his family gatherings and celebrations, and I tried to be a part of them. But, it didn't feel right for either of us. We both knew this relationship would soon be over. At that time, there didn't seem to be much support or acceptance for blending religions within a family. We didn't find any answers or encouragement from the rabbi his father had sent us to see. Out of respect for each other, we decided we would have to go our separate ways. Although his footsteps were good ones, my son would not follow in them, and I would not be the mother of his children.

He made a promise to me he would only date or marry Jewish women after me. I believe he kept that promise. We are still friends today.

Birthday Tribute

Jesse

We admire and appreciate you for:

your intelligence, your ability to have fun,

your deep love for your daughter Juliet,

your ability to rebound and climb like Spiderman,

saying "yes" to life,

your sense of humor, your open mind, your compassion,

your love for animals, your confidence, your love of music,

your extreme mathematical intelligence,

and your beautiful, artistic mind.

We turn to you for:

your technical expertise,

and the warmest most loving embrace any human being could ever hope for.

You make a difference to us and to the world because:

you remind us of the importance of asking questions,

you love deeply, you are able to have fun,

you have the ability to inspire us through music and your passion,

and you aim for the stars.

You have taught us:

to appreciate the concept of "Ferris Bueller's Day Off,"

and to truly be able to love.

Special Memories We Have Shared:

You hanging on your dad's arm and flying/racing through the snow.

Your birth was the start of a new generation for our family

and when you came into our world, we learned many things from you—

most importantly how to love by looking beyond ourselves.

Our first trip to Disneyland was made special by you helping us to all be kids again.

You looking up at the stars and singing to Juliet.

Our special memories are made every day with every moment we spend together.

We love you, Jesse

Happy Birthday from your Family

Grandma's Rings

Joy

Our relationship, daughter and dad, had existed in an uneasy truce for many years.

He left our family—my mom, my two sisters, and me—in 1959. I was in fourth grade and the oldest of three girls. He had attempted to see us for a year or so after that, and then he just moved on to another place, another family. We were left behind, with no money or child support from him. Our mom was ill. We lived with very little money and no car.

Thankfully, our mom made sure we kept our house. It was a house on a street with a good bus line. Keeping that house was an incredible gift.

We lived in a wonderful south Minneapolis neighborhood full of lakes, a creek, a waterfall, and the Mississippi River—a neighborhood where kids could go out in the morning, play all day, come home for meals, and go out again until dark. In the summer, you could get on your bike and ride to the falls to meet your friends. You could gather the neighborhood kids together, dress up, and put on a parade or a backyard play. Although it was a neighborhood within a big city, the local dairy milk truck still delivered milk to your house. For summer birthday parties, they would give you and your friends a ride in a special horse-drawn birthday wagon. In the winter, you could go ice-skating at the neighborhood rink after school, walk to the library, or to your piano lessons taught by a neighbor lady.

We were the baby-boomer generation. There were lots of kids. We formed groups of friends. We planned our own activities and made our own fun. Parents were there in our world to supply food and shelter but not to plan our every activity. Looking back, this helped us to develop the obvious social skills, but it did more than that. Playing together then helped us to learn how to eventually work together. We learned what it took to organize groups, plan activities, how to get from "point A" to "point B," how to lead, and how to rely on ourselves. We learned, through trial and error, what worked and what didn't when it came to being and keeping friends. Life-long lessons were learned in how to communicate with each other and who we could count on.

It was a safer, simpler time and place. The people in the neighborhood were mostly Scandinavian in heritage and Lutheran in religion (with a few Catholics thrown into the mix). Most of us went to the public schools in the neighborhood. We walked to school with our friends carrying our books, sloshing through the snow and slipping on the ice in winter and stopping to smell the lilacs in the spring.

It was an urban neighborhood of middle-class families in a time before people moved to the suburbs—mostly two parent families. It was embarrassing in the 1960s to tell people your parents were divorced. It was embarrassing to say that your dad didn't support you or that you were poor. It was embarrassing that you didn't hear from your dad on your birthday. Sometimes, I just told people he was dead. It was easier.

He attempted to see my sisters and me again when we were adults. We accepted him back into our lives in a casual acquaintance sort of way. It made it easier for our grandparents. He was their only child, and we were the grandchildren they loved.

And so, the uneasy truce was held for many years. We never asked him for anything. Somehow, we still hoped that he loved us, that he had always loved us, and that he would show us his love. We hoped he would try to make amends and that that would be enough for us to forgive the years of abandonment.

Grandpa died in 1989 after a slow decline into Alzheimer's. Grandma bravely went on trying to live an independent life after sixty-three years of being a partner to Grandpa. Then, in 2000, after ninety-two years on the planet, Grandma died. I feel so lucky to have known the wondrous love of a grandma for forty-eight years of my life. My sisters and I had felt her unconditional, unwavering love for us every day of our lives.

When she died, I had just finished treatment for breast cancer. I had survived the surgeries, chemo, and radiation, and I was putting my life back together. I never told my grandma I had cancer. She would have worried so. I needed to spare her that worry.

Dawn and I got on a plane in Tucson and rushed to Minneapolis for Grandma's funeral. We went directly to Dad's apartment. I wanted to feel her presence, to think of her in her alive days, and to still feel Grandma's love with me.

• • • • • •

Grandma had immigrated to the United States in 1917, with her parents and her sisters. She had worked all of her life, mostly as a seamstress in a factory, sewing drapes with knuckles crooked from arthritis, but always with manicured hands and pink nail polish. She always wore her wedding rings with pride. Her hands held my hands and my sisters' hands when we were small. Her hands cradled our faces. She made meals and cleaned up after us with those hands.

As the years went on, she and Grandpa gave up all of their homes, cars, and most of their possessions. The last time I saw her was in a room in an assisted living facility. She was somewhat confused, but she knew me and called me "her Joy." I tried to tidy up the room for her and organize the few clothes and things she had left. When I opened the drawer in her bedside table, I found a drawer full of photographs.

Here, in the drawer right next to her, were her most important possessions, the memories of all of those she had loved. There were old photos of her parents, her sisters, her husband, her son, and her grandchildren. There were more recent photos of her great-grandchildren. We were all there close to her.

There was one that she had taken of my sisters and me on

Christmas Eve in 1958. Christmas Eve was always the special holiday night that we spent with her and Grandpa. She was so excited to cook us a dinner and to have us all at the table she had carefully set with her holiday dishes. She and Grandpa watched with anticipation as we opened the special gifts they had picked out for us. We, her three granddaughters, were her pride and joy. We always knew that she and Grandpa loved us. We never doubted it for a second. They told us, and they showed us.

There we were in this photo, three sisters together. Sisters—a meshing of hearts, souls, and the mystical chords of our shared memories. We were in their living room, in front of the Christmas tree, and each proudly showing off our just-opened Christmas presents—new musical instruments. Bonnie was holding a Mickey Mouse guitar, pretending to strum it, and proudly showing off her wrist with her new Mickey Mouse watch. Dawn was smiling from ear to ear, her dimples showing, and sitting at a little toy piano complete with sheet music. And there I was in my new, blue velvet dress, holding my first real musical instrument—an accordion.

I had wanted to play the piano. My parents weren't quite ready to get such a large instrument for such a little girl. They told me if I showed them I could stick with it and succeed at playing a smaller instrument, they would "think about" getting me a piano. And so, one night every week for about a year, my dad drove me downtown to the music school where he took his voice lessons. While he was downstairs singing, the seven-year-old me hauled that accordion up the narrow staircase to the classroom upstairs and studied until I could almost make music with it. The next year, I got the piano.

Here, in this small assisted living room she now lived in, she was still proudly wearing her wedding ring set on her finger. Their monetary worth was very small, but their value to me had nothing to do with money.

• • • • • •

I had not asked him for anything since the day he left us. But, now I needed to. And so, as we sat in his apartment, distributing the photographs she had lovingly kept in her drawer and discussing the final arrangements she had made for herself, I summoned the courage to ask him what he had done with her rings.

He said that he had put them in a safe deposit box belonging to his third ex-wife.

I asked, "Could I see them, Dad?" I wanted to remember her hands when she was alive.

He didn't respond.

I said, "Dad, please make sure that when something happens to you, those rings stay in our family."

That's when he said he might need them if he got married again, or he might need to sell them to pay for Grandma's funeral expenses.

I knew that would not be what Grandma wanted. That was it for me, the old "straw that broke the camel's back." I could no longer keep the truce with him.

And so, once again, we were estranged.

Love and Commitment

Dawn

Here we were again, my little son and I, the two of us trying to find our way through life. As he grew, I noticed he began to take on a protective role. He started to look over my shoulder from the back seat of the car and tell me when we were getting low on gas. He called me on it if I was driving too fast. I watched as this little man began to emerge.

I did start to go out. But, as my mother had been when she was a single mom, I was selective about the men I introduced to my child. I didn't want him to go through any more heartache over my breakups.

He was just beginning to develop a long distance relationship with his biological father, but it was an intermittent relationship and always had our "two rules" attached to it.

The first rule was: never lean on him, because you might fall on your facc. The second rule was: seize the moment, and enjoy him while you can, because he will soon be gone. These were my rules. They were the survival skills that I had developed, early in life, for my relationship with my dad. I found they also applied in my relationship with my son's father.

I tried to fill the gap for Jesse, as my mother had done for me. I tried to protect him from disappointment and hurt. What I learned, through trial and error, was that some things were out of my control. I could not fix feelings and emotions felt by someone else. I could not take away the hurt caused by someone else. What I could do was help my son develop coping skills, help him build his self-confidence, and provide him with an environment full of unconditional love.

I had to get busy. I needed to get serious about my career while continuing to be able to support my son and myself. I got a great new job as a stylist in the best salon in town. I began to develop a new group of friends. And from them, I met the men I would have in my future.

I was trying to discover what was important to me and how to navigate through it all to find the right relationship. I was trying to discover not only what *I* wanted, but who would be right for my son.

I met a wonderful man from Italy. He was a great dancer, and his accent alone made me smile. We had fun together, but he was a guy I could only envision as staying single for the near future. Our time together was intense but short, yet it had value. I will always remember him, but I never introduced him to my son.

My next love was a man unlike anyone I had ever met before. He was much older than I was, incredibly warm, and had a great relationship with his children and his ex-wife. I thought he was the one.

I felt safer with him than I ever had with anyone before. I could sleep in the car while he drove. That had never happened to me before. I had always been a nervous passenger.

One evening he called to ask me out to dinner. I thought this might be the time he would ask me what I wanted to hear from him. We went to a steak and seafood restaurant that I had not been to before. He was a meat and potatoes kind of guy. He wore cardigan sweaters and smoked a pipe. As we sat in our big half-circle booth snuggled together, I thought to myself that I needed this warmth in my life. I deserved this man. I adored him, and he seemed to adore me.

When dinner was over and the dessert we had shared was gone, he held my hand tightly and with tears in his eyes told me why he could not spend his life with me. He had been seeing another woman, someone closer to his own age. He was terrified of the difference in our ages. He wanted a safe bet. Feeling safe wasn't only important to me. It was important to him, too.

I must have been swerving slightly as I drove home alone that night. A policeman pulled me over. He came to my window and asked me if everything was okay. I was crying too hard to see what he looked like. But, he seemed to understand me when I told him, "No, everything is not okay."

He told me to turn off my car. Then he got into the passenger seat and listened while I told him what had just happened. He said he thought the guy was a fool, and that someday he would regret breaking up with me. I listened to him as he told me someone would come my way who was just right for me and my son, and we would be just right for him, too. We talked until he could see that I was alright to drive, and then he let me go. Talk about protect and serve. He was my guardian angel that night.

I was tired of heartache. When a friend asked me if I would go out with her cousin, a Marine who was home from duty, I said, "No."

She tried everything she could to convince me. She described him as a muscular and handsome man—who was also the gentlest person she had ever known.

I said, "No way, I am not interested in going out with anyone."

We finally agreed that a group of us would go out together.

At first, I thought that this guy, Michael, was stuck up and rude. What I found out later was that he was extremely shy and had just been too nervous to talk to me. Over the next year, we got to know each other through letters and long distance phone calls. When he could get leave, he would drive all night in his little Fiat convertible from California to Arizona to see us. It was always *us* from the beginning with him. We did things, just the two of us, when *I* wanted to. But when it was *his* idea, we did things he knew my son would enjoy, like going to the zoo. We were both falling in love with him.

It was difficult having him far away. I was a working, single mom with responsibilities, but I also wanted to go out occasionally. I made it clear to him I wasn't ready to have our relationship be exclusive. I really didn't think our long-distance relationship could work. He was two years younger than I was, and our lives had been very different. There seemed to me to be gaps between us that I didn't think we could overcome.

I told him I wanted to break up because I didn't think it was fair to him to be strung along in a relationship that could never work. He was just beginning his military career and had the chance to go anywhere and do anything that he wanted. A relationship with me would mean instant parenting and commitment. I told him I wanted to see other people. I tried to convince him that we were not right for him.

As I spoke, he listened without comment, but I could see my words were hurting him. When it was his turn to speak, he told me he understood what I was saying, but that he felt differently. He said he loved me, that no matter what he would always love me, and the way he looked at it he was getting two for the price of one—a sort of head start on a family. And, a family is what he wanted. He said he would wait for me.

Over the next few months, I was torn up inside. My Italian man showed up again, and I thought that seeing him might be just what I needed. Over dinner, I told him about this Marine of mine, and what he had said to me.

He looked at me and said, "Dawn, that kind of love doesn't come around very often. I care about you very much—you mean a lot to me—but you may want to consider marrying this guy."

The next time I saw Michael was when I visited him in southern California. I was on a business trip but was able to spend a few days with him sightseeing. As we drove from San Diego across the bridge on our way to dinner at the Coronado Boathouse restaurant, I looked at him and realized just how much I had missed him. It was becoming clear to me that love and commitment were really one and the same for me. This is what I had been looking for. I did love this man, and for once in my life I was in love with someone who loved me back in a way that might mean forever. Someone who would say what I needed to hear—what I must have been waiting for.

As we sat at the big table on the top floor of the restaurant looking out over the water, he said, "Will you marry me?"

I said, "Yes."

We were married in Tucson, during one of the strongest monsoon storms I have ever experienced. I took it to be a good sign. I had heard that it's supposed to be good luck for it to rain on your wedding day. If that is true, we received a lot of good luck that day.

I realized later that my wedding day was on the same date in August that I had boarded that plane years before and left Minneapolis for my new life in Tucson. I took this to be a good sign, too.

I gathered together these signs of good luck, searching for some kind of proof our marriage would survive. Over the years, I had seen many marriages go bad. As a child of divorce, I doubted the survival of *any* marriage, not just my own. I just didn't have much faith in the idea that a marriage could last a lifetime.

Saying goodbye to my job, my family, and my friends in Tucson, Jesse and I joined Michael in California. The first year of our marriage did not turn out as we had planned. During our first week in our new home, Michael received orders to go overseas—unaccompanied. He was going to Japan for a year without us.

We tried to make the best of the time we had before he would leave us. We spent time at the beach and took Jesse to Disneyland, but there was always the underlying reality that we would soon be separated.

I didn't know what to do. I had just left my life in Tucson, and it would have felt strange and sad to go right back without Michael. During our last days in California, my lifelong friend, Kim, came to visit us and said, "Why don't you come back to Minneapolis?" I jumped at the chance.

Kim and I rented a house together for what would end up being my two years back home. As a good best friend would do, she took me to dinner on my first wedding anniversary—in place of my husband who was so far away.

Meanwhile, my marriage was surviving through letters and expensive, international, long distance phone calls.

During my second year back home, Kim found out she was going to be a mother. I felt so blessed to be able to share this experience with my dear friend. I was her labor coach and was able to experience childbirth and early motherhood with her. We decided that to her beautiful little daughter, my name would forever be "Auntie Dawn." The time we shared was one of the richest times of my life. It reminded me of how much I loved babies, and that I wanted more of my own.

When Michael returned, we wanted stability. Together we decided the best place to put down our roots was back in Tucson. We wanted to be near the support of both of our families. We had a short window of time in which to move with the military, so we were soon on our way back to the desert. While it was hard to leave Kim and her daughter, I knew they would always be just a plane flight or phone call away. Our friendship was timeless.

It didn't take long to find my way back to the best salon in town, and I quickly settled in with my old group of friends. Michael landed a position in local law enforcement and continued his military service in the reserves. It was now time for us to grow our family.

Birthday Tribute

Michael

As a young boy, you waited for the taxi to bring your Dad home, and you were so proud as he emerged in his Air Force uniform.

You have happy memories of life growing up in Spain, Italy and many U.S. cities.

Your Mom and Dad were proud of you when you emerged from boot camp in your Marine Corp's dress blues.

Now, you are happiest when you are:
watching the U of A Wildcats win,
holding the remote in your hand,
working out in your weight room,
taking a nap,
driving in your MG with the top down,
home with your family,
or watching your children shine.

Although you now wear a different uniform
(the Tucson uniform of tank tops and shorts),
we are proud of you, because to us you are

The World's Best Dad.

• • • • • •

Our son Bryan was born the following August. How different it was having a baby with a husband who could share in the joys of parenting with me from the beginning. I found that I fell in love with Michael all over again as I watched him play with and care for our children. What a beautiful boy, our Bryan, full of energy, his blue eyes bright with excitement and wonder.

This was a busy time, and we found that we had done the right thing by moving closer to our families. It really did take a village to keep our family going. Michael and I were both busy working full-time jobs (with various shifts and weekend work) as well as taking college classes. We would never have been able to do it all without the help of our families.

We found the perfect house. It had a small, attached guest house for my mom to live in, an exercise room for Michael, a pool for the kids, and a fireplace for me. This perfect-for-us house became the place for our family celebrations, provided a place for my mom to retire, and became home to an endless variety of pets. It was a place for us to grow.

Birthday Tribute

Bryan

A kick boxer in the womb, you learned to run before you walked. Walking was way too slow for you. We admire your commitment to health and physical fitness. Your dad is especially proud, that you have followed in his footsteps as a Work-Out King. Your dad and mom always say your voice only has one volume, loud. You have used your voice to speak up for yourself and others, to get where you need to be, and to protect the unprotected.

You are an incredibly talented and gifted artist; your ability to express yourself in your drawings is awe-inspiring. We admire your commitment to learning to speak Japanese in order to further your goal of going to Japan.

A stealth risk taker, you are sensitive enough to tell your mom what you do after you do it (so that she would not worry).

From Bam-Bam to Batman, you are incredibility strong, both physically and in character. To your little sister you will always be Weebee.

The Bruce Wayne in you enjoys the latest toys, costumes, and collectibles. From the age of two and your first costume as a clown, to wanting to go ice skating in your Frosty the Snow Man costume, to your Mighty Morphin Power Rangers and Pokémon, we have always enjoyed your excitement and surprises.

You found your soul mate at a young age, and have been loyal and steadfast in your love for Pilar. Your honor and commitment is yet again, inspirational.

You are: handsome and smart, passionate and grateful, sweet and gentle, strong and compassionate, dedicated and loyal.

The truth is - if Batman were real, *he* would want to be you.

• • • • • •

Where did the time go? All of a sudden, it seemed, Jesse was turning 18 and moving into his own apartment. What would we do with this empty room? I set out to finally have a home office. Maybe I would do some writing or have a quiet place to read. I pulled up the carpet (that was once the place my teenager spilled everything on), painted the room, and put down a new floor. I started to look through magazines and catalogs, trying to decide on furniture to fill this new space I had created.

I thought I had worn myself out. Our boys, along with the normal, everyday housework; cooking; my full-time job; and part-time school, kept me very busy. Now, on the weekends I was redoing this room. It was time for a check-up anyway, so I made an appointment to see my doctor.

When she told me that I was tired because I was going to have a baby at 40 years old, I fell into the chair in disbelief. Could I do this again? Could my husband do this again? We had given away all of our baby things long ago (thinking of course that we wouldn't need them anymore). When I called home to tell Michael the news, you would have thought I had told him we had just won the lottery. I could hear him jumping up and down with excitement.

It took me a little longer to get my head around this about-face that was before me. I was the one who would be going through the physical part, and I had concerns due to my age. Would this baby be healthy? I had to know. I decided to have all of the tests my doctor suggested, and thankfully they all indicated the baby was healthy. When they told me I was going to have a girl this time, I was overcome with a deep sense of fulfillment. Somehow, my life had come full circle.

I was glad that I had chosen a neutral color scheme for the room which would now become a nursery. We prepared for our third decade of parenting.

Having had the opportunity to raise two boys was a wonderful gift. I learned so much from them. As they went through their childhoods, I got to experience mine again through their eyes—through the eyes of boys. Without sons, I would never in my life have been asked to play quarterback or been given lizards as gifts. I would never have felt that I had my own personal soldiers, as they grew to be strong, incredible men watching over me.

This time we were having a girl, our daughter, Molly Marie. Because she was supposed to be born on Saint Patrick's Day, we thought a good Irish name was in order (even though neither one of us is Irish). She was born just two days, but nineteen years, from her brother Jesse's birthday.

In the delivery room, my doctor asked Michael (at the last minute) if he wanted to help deliver her. Of course he did. My BFF Kim called the hospital just as Molly was being born. I put the phone next to me so that she could be with us. As my husband brought our daughter to me to hold, I fell in love again.

Kim flew from Minneapolis to be with me in Tucson when Molly and I came home from the hospital. We spent the next week holding her and staring at her in amazement, as if we had never seen a baby before.

When Kim left, my mom and I shared time with Molly and again stared in amazement. I asked my mom if she felt the same overwhelming love for her that I felt.

She said, "I love her with all of my heart. I would die for her tomorrow, if I had to. But I get my true happiness from seeing how happy she makes you."

I had no idea then that what she said to me would prepare me for becoming a grandmother myself, soon.

Over the coming years, I watched as Joy parented Molly also, as if she were her own. When I found out I was going to be a mom again, I asked Joy if she would help me. I would need her even more this time. I wanted to continue in my career, and I wanted to be sure that my children had the love and guidance they needed from all of us, our family. Joy had a busy professional life, also. But I thought that between the two of us, Molly would have a full-time mom. I asked Joy for that commitment before Molly was born, and without hesitation she said, "Absolutely."

Molly became the center of all of our worlds. This little girl belongs to all of us.

To say that Joy has lived up to her commitment would be an understatement. What my sister has given me, through this process of growing our family together, is the peace of mind that most parents don't have. I know if something ever happened to me, my daughter would still have someone in the mother's role, someone who would step into my shoes without question. Because of the added help and support Joy gave, I could enjoy parenting for another decade. At the same time, Joy could be a parent, too. It was a win-win. She has definitely earned her

Mother's Day cards.

As we did with our sons, Michael and I spent the first ten years of Molly's life learning how to have another human being depend on us and on our time.

We are currently experiencing the second decade—the one where we learn how to let her go. The one when we have to learn how to let her be independent.

She is independent, but not in the reckless way that I was at her age. She knows how to make good choices. She is becoming a confidant, beautiful young woman, who will hopefully fulfill her childhood commitment from the Powerpuff Girls to "save the universe before bedtime."

When Molly begins to date, I trust she will think it through, as she does with everything, and choose someone—not just accept someone because he has chosen her. I hope that she chooses someone who cherishes her, yet challenges her to be her best.

My children have all experienced different phases in my growth as a parent. With Jesse, I was in my twenties and just growing up myself. For much of his childhood, I was a single mom. It was just the two of us.

Bryan probably got the more traditional mom. I was in my thirties, with a loving marriage and a home. With the addition of Michael's parents and siblings, he had two families for love and support.

Now, with Molly, I'm an older, more experienced parent—if only to realize just how fast it all goes. Now, it is more important to me to let the dishes sit while we talk at the table. The dishes will get done, and maybe we'll even do them together. I will stop to watch her new dance line routine when I get home, no matter how tired I might be. Because soon, before I know it, she will be grown.

Birthday Tribute

Molly

♥

We admire and appreciate you for:

your hard work, dedication and stamina,

your ability to find humor in each day, your spontaneity,

your integrity, your love for animals, your love of reading,

your kindness and compassion, your thoughtfulness,

and making the needs of others important to you.

We turn to you for:

friendship, a beach-buddy and traveling companion,

your eagerness to spend time with those you love,

your laughter and having fun.

You make a difference to us and the world because:

your devotion is deep, you choose to do the right thing,

your commitment to your success and the success of others

shows your ability to lead.

You have taught us:

to remember to laugh, and a deeper meaning of to love and cherish.

Special Memories We Have Shared:

taking you to kindergarten and staying there with you in class,

our pride in watching your performances as you have grown into a dancer,

taking you to baton classes, piano lessons and to visit your teachers,

catching sand dollars at The Del, relaxing on the sun deck, and watching the ocean together.

The years go by so fast, so please make 15 last (for as long as you can).

We love you, Molly

Happy Birthday from your Family

• • • • • •

I have always worried that my three children, born in different decades, wouldn't be close to each other because of the enormous gaps in their ages. I envied other families, the ones who had children who were close together in age, because those children had built in playmates.

Now, I get my greatest joy from watching my almost all grown up children hang out together, and from hanging out with them myself. They have become friends in their own ways. Although they were children at different times, they are definitely siblings.

• • • • • •

Molly did get a built-in playmate, when her brother Jesse's daughter, Juliet, was born. Molly became an aunt when she was only one-and-a-half years old, and she and her niece are growing up together. They have each other to share things with, and they have each other to talk to.

My granddaughter, Juliet, has added so much to all of our lives. I love to watch as Molly and Juliet laugh and have fun, or text each other when they are not together. I love it when I receive a text from Juliet just to ask "What's up?" or a text to tell me how she is doing or feeling, or just to say "Good night. I love you, Gramma." The time we spend with her is priceless.

Birthday Tribute

Juliet

J is for joining the ranks of teenagers. You are now 13!

U is for the uncanny ability you have for lighting up the room just by walking in.

L is for the love we all have for you.

I is for the incredible girl you are.

E is for the excitement you bring to our world.

T is for the time we cherish by sharing it with you.

To us you are:

the Pancake Princess (you can eat more of these than most Sumo wrestlers),

the Queen of Chocolate (you never met a piece of chocolate you didn't like),

the only broken-footed body surfer on the California coast,

a lover of animals big and small,

our miracle.

The Ex-Husband and Adventures in Dating

Joy

Why did I choose him? He was a man who smoked cigarettes and drank every night. But, I accepted him for who he was. He had qualities that I valued. So, I overlooked the smoking and drinking for many years, until a time came when they could no longer be overlooked. He had been married once several years before, and he had maintained a nurturing relationship with his two daughters. I admired that. He had always paid his child support, and he was committed to putting both daughters through college. All of the things that my own dad had never done, but I had always wished he had.

We found a lot of common ground. We were both intellectually curious people, eager to learn new things, life-long learners. We both valued our solitude and our alone time. We knew how to give each other space. We both loved to travel. And boy did we travel. We had many great adventures in Hong Kong, China, Macau, Japan, Brazil, England, Ireland, Scotland,

Wales, France, Germany, Switzerland, Austria, Holland, and Russia and Armenia (when they were part of the Soviet Union).

We had been together for 18 years when I was diagnosed with breast cancer.

How did cancer happen to me? I was only forty-seven. I had always taken good care of myself. I had been a vegetarian since I was 18. I didn't smoke or drink. There was no family history of breast cancer that I could pin this on. This wasn't supposed to happen—but it did. I now had to absorb all of the information from the doctors about treatment options, drug side effects, and mortality rates. I had to make decisions, very important decisions, based on the information we gathered. Eventually, you begin to understand that this can happen to anyone, at anytime. It's a crap-shoot. One day you are fine, going along happily busy in your day-to-day life. The next day, you are told that you have cancer. It's a shock that changes you.

At first, he was the model husband and caregiver. He went to every doctor's appointment with me, asked questions, and took notes. My breast cancer became a project for him. Once a mechanical engineer, always a mechanical engineer. That was how his brain worked. Here's a problem; let's fix it. Then, as the months of treatment went on, and I was sick from the treatment, very sick, day after day, he got angry with me. Angry that he couldn't fix it, I think. I didn't need anger. I needed more than he could give me. He blamed me for the illness. It was disrupting his life.

As he drank every night and his anger surfaced, I found myself not only uncomfortable in my own body from the cancer treatment but uncomfortable in my own home. A home that once was a peaceful place of refuge for me no longer was.

Many days during this time, in the depths of my feelings of despair, I would visualize myself at my favorite place by the ocean—The Hotel del Coronado in California. I would see the sunlight sparkle off of the blue water, hear the roar of the waves, and smell the sea breeze. I would see myself walking along this beach of golden sand and feel at peace. I promised myself when I got through this, I'd go back to my peaceful get-away place and walk up to the ocean's shore, listen to the waves, smell the salt air, and know that I would be well.

I did find the love and support I needed, but it came from other people. Some amazing people did amazing things for me during this time. I had my family and friends. They were there for me. I came to rely on them and their love instead of on him. Some of this love came from people I hadn't known well, or even at all, before this happened. They were able to be there, but he was not.

We were drifting apart to our separate spaces more and more. We were no longer happy together. I started to feel that maybe I had stayed too long at the fair.

He started asking me for a divorce as soon as I'd finished radiation. He had given up on our marriage. And, I didn't know how to fix it. My body was weak and exhausted from treatment. I resisted the idea of divorce for several months. I never wanted to be a divorced woman. That is what happened to my mom. It wasn't supposed to happen to me. But, it did. In the end, his alcohol-infused anger turned into isolation. It overwhelmed us, and I knew the good we'd had was gone. Our marriage, our partnership in life, was over. I had to close the door and move on.

The drive for self-preservation kicked in. I gathered my assets, built a new home for myself, and moved to a new neighborhood. I was starting again.

After the first few months of putting my new life in place, I was driving down the road in front of my house to meet a friend for lunch, and I felt as if I'd been let out of prison. My body was healing from the cancer treatment. My spirit was becoming whole again. I no longer had to walk on eggshells around him. I no longer had to fear that I would anger him and then get the silent treatment for days. I had freedom to do what I wanted to do. I could make my own choices. His voice left my head. I was me again.

• • • • • •

Finding myself single again was unexpected. I hadn't planned for it. Although I do enjoy the freedom that comes with being single, I also miss having a man in my life to love. So, eventually, I began dating. I really wasn't prepared for this.

I eased into it slowly by rekindling a romance from before I was married. He was a friend from familiar territory.

Then, I ventured out into new territory. There was the guy who had no furniture in his living room and no stove to cook on in the kitchen. But, he was a musician and seemed so nice. One night I made dinner for him and brought it to his house. While we were eating my home-made broccoli quiche with rice pilaf, the discussion turned to politics.

Oh, it started innocently enough. We were talking about music. He asked me who some of my musical influences had been over the years. I mentioned several. However, when I said I had always loved the songs of Jackson Browne, he became quite animated. He said he loved everything about Jackson Browne, *except* his politics. I should have stopped there, but of course I started expressing my own views. Turns out he was turned off by my liberal ways. It seems that he was just getting in on the ground floor of a new political party—a party which was to the right of the right wing. It's a good thing we didn't get any further. That could have gotten really messy.

There was another guy who seemed nice. We met at a cafe. He was into real estate and yoga. I'm into real estate and yoga! It turned out that he was way more into his cats as companions than into me.

I met my Sweet Southern Boy through an online dating site. We had our core values in common—at least the ones that this dating site measured. It seemed as if we were the perfect match.

He had grown up in the southern U.S. and had impeccable sweet, southern manners. He opened car doors for me. He loved to cook and made gourmet meals in my kitchen. On Sunday mornings, he served me perfect omelets on plates that he insisted be warmed in the oven. He liked to do things to please me. He loved to travel, and he wanted me to join him. We took several trips together, including a glorious week in San Francisco, riding cable cars, eating vegetarian sushi, having drinks at the Top of the Mark while watching the breathtaking sunset over the city below us, and sharing a late night Irish coffee at the legendary Buena Vista Cafe along Fisherman's Wharf. He'd once been a professional photographer and had a keen eye for detail. He saw art in everything. He loved, as I did, to go to museums and galleries. On top of all of this, he was extremely good-looking in what I thought to be a Robert Redford sort of way. I fell for him deeply.

Looking back, of course, there were signs I should have paid attention to. But, I so enjoyed being with him that I wanted to believe in this relationship. So, I found ways, as people often do, to explain these signs away.

The first sign was that he was in his mid-50s and not only had he never been married, he had never even lived with a girlfriend. Of course, I told myself that this meant that he had just been waiting for me.

The second sign was that he lived with his mother. Of course, I told myself that this meant he was a caring, loving, devoted son taking care of his widowed mother.

As our relationship grew, he invited me to meet his mother. He planned to cook a wonderful dinner for us at their home. I arrived and chatted with her in the living room while my Sweet Southern Boy was cooking in his kitchen. When he came into the living room to join us, his mother told him bluntly that he had nicer jeans than the ones he was wearing. She then told him to go change his clothes. I tried to cut the tension and relieve the humiliation I imagined he must be feeling by saying that he looked great to me (which, of course, he did). The reaction I was expecting was that he would stand up to her. Or, maybe he would simply ignore her. But, without hesitation and without saying a word, he went into his bedroom and changed his jeans. I was shocked. I couldn't imagine what would make a grown man do that.

We had been together for several months when he called me one night to say he'd signed me up to bring a salad to a potluck for a party the next weekend. Oh good, he was finally going to introduce me to his co-workers! That would be another step forward in our relationship. He said no that it wasn't a party at his work, it was a party at his club. I thought, wow—a country club! He then told me a secret that even his mother didn't know about him. He was a nudist. That tidbit wasn't included in his online profile on the dating website.

The party was at a nudist club. I asked a few questions and found out he wasn't just one of those people who might like to skinny dip in the pool occasionally. He wasn't one of those people who just liked to relax around his house without a lot of clothes on to weigh him down. He belonged to a nudist club, and this party was their weekly potluck. I thought to myself that this was the one place he could be where his mother couldn't tell him what to wear.

He talked about a future in which he wanted to vacation at nudist resorts all around the world. I began to realize his plan wasn't just to attend an occasional potluck. He wanted to go to a nudist resort where every event, including grocery shopping for the ingredients to take to the potluck, was "clothing optional." I pondered the advantage of this type of travel for a minute. You definitely would have less to pack. You could probably even get by with just a carry-on for a trip to France.

But I couldn't go with him to the potluck or to the resorts around the world. This wasn't a lifestyle I was interested in or a club I wanted to join. I couldn't change myself to be with him. When I am invited to a party, I like to think about what I'm going to wear. I like to dress for special events. Maybe I'll even go shopping and get a new outfit. I'm definitely into fashion as a part of the event.

We went on together trying to make our relationship work. I think he really did want to be with me. We both accepted that he would go alone to his club events. Eventually the inevitable happened. He met a woman who *was* willing to join the nudist club. We broke up. My heart was broken. We got back together and broke up again several times over the next year. Finally, after a lot of drama and heartbreak, I needed to get off the breakup roller coaster. It just had to be over.

Several months after the last breakup, I found a Sunday edition of *The New York Times* on my doorstep. I don't subscribe to *The New York Times*, but as an avid newspaper reader, I read it page by page, savoring every article in this icon of newspapers. There, on the first page of the Travel section, was a big article on nudist vacations—complete with photos. And yes, there was a photo of someone who looked just like my Sweet Southern Boy, front and center, playing volleyball in the pool. His face was turned slightly, but I recognized his profile and every inch of his body.

I don't know how the paper got delivered to my house that day. He denied knowing anything about it, but I suspect that he may know how and why I received it.

A few months later, he asked me to have dinner with him. As I sat across the table, eating my veggie lo mein with crispy noodles, he told me the reason for this dinner. He wanted to tell me in person that he was now engaged to the nudist girlfriend. See, if that had been me, I'd be out shopping for the perfect wedding dress.

I wonder what she wore.

So, once again I find myself single and *still* looking.

The Road

Dawn

How many times had I driven down this road? It was the path that took me from the Lake Nokomis neighborhood where I grew up, to the Uptown neighborhood where I lived as a young adult. It seemed almost everyone lived in Uptown in their twenties. It was a sort of rite of passage.

Uptown was where the trendy restaurants were located in the city during the 1970s. I waited tables, as did most of my friends. It was a great way to always have money in your pocket. Jobs were easy to get, and being a "people person," waiting tables suited me. It also meant I could work at night and hang out at the lake with my friends all day, all summer. That was what Minnesota summers were all about.

Living in Minneapolis during my late teen years was a carefree time. I shared the top floor of an old mansion with four friends, and most of the time we worked at the same restaurant. So, if one of your roommates needed the money more than you did at the moment, she would work your shift for you in exchange for you working her next shift.

I learned a lot in Uptown—how to cook, what friendship meant, that I wasn't a morning person, and that I fell in love hard. I learned that what was really important would never go away.

I am driving this street as a guest of my city now. I'm visiting my BFF Kim and my sister Joy, who is renting an apartment here again for the summer. Joy has had my daughter Molly with her for the past couple of weeks, for company and to show Molly, a girl born in the Tucson desert, what a Minnesota summer is all about. I am driving this city street to pick them up again today, as I have for the past few days since I arrived.

I have taken notice on this street of things familiar, and how many things have changed. The city seems smaller than I remember—not the city as a whole, but the things in it. The street lights, for instance, weren't they higher? The streets themselves seem so much narrower than I remember. How did I ever drive in the winter, when snow banks lined them and made them narrower still? How do these Minnesotans still do it? At least during the energy crisis of the 1970s a lot of us were driving Volkswagen Beetles or some other type of compact car. People are now maneuvering SUVs through these streets! I guess the winter driving skills developed by most Minnesotans carry through to the summer.

The summer, thank God for summers in Minnesota when everything comes alive again. It is so green. It almost seems fake to me after living in the pastels of the Arizona desert for the past 30 years. As I pull into the caramel corn drive-up (that I can't believe looks exactly the same after all of these years) I think to myself: Only in Minnesota. Do they pipe the scent of this caramel corn out into the street on purpose? It is simply impossible to just drive by.

I am happy as a clam now driving along, popping kernels in my mouth, and getting lost in thought. I know this street. It is familiar. It is at that moment I look to the right, and I see the words "The Walker." I don't remember consciously turning into the parking lot, but here I am. I am in the parking lot of the building where I think my dad is living. My sister, Bonnie, had told me that he was here, and that he was very old and ill. She thought he might be dying. I remember thinking—no actually deciding—I wasn't going to care. Why should I? He had never cared about me or my sisters. I had given him so many opportunities to be the dad I had wanted or the dad I sometimes pretended he was. It had never worked. He just couldn't be that man. He was not capable of it. He didn't have it in him, anywhere. I still have a hard time understanding how he could have possibly been the son of my grandpa, who was so wonderful and loving. I thought Grandpa was Santa Claus—the real one. I guess it skipped a generation.

What do I do now? As I try to figure out why I am even in the parking lot, I realize that I am wiping a stream of tears from my face. They are simply pouring from me. I don't want to be here. I want to go have fun. That is what this trip is about for me. Why am I here?

I knew I would go in. As I walked through the lobby, I said

to myself: Of course, you dummy, here you go again. You are a glutton for punishment. You are setting yourself up grand this time for the inevitable mule-kick to the gut feeling that he will eventually leave you with, and you know it. But here you are being good old Dawn, the one who forgives even the evilest of men in her life. Here you go again.

The man at the desk on the first floor looks at me curiously when I say, "I think my dad might be here."

I feel compelled to explain to him that I don't know why I am here, that it has been a long time since I have seen him, and I probably should not be here. He steers me toward the elevator and says, "He is here. He's on the second floor. Why don't you just go up and see how it goes?"

Sure, he probably had a dad who loved him, a dad who cared if he had food to eat and something new to wear for the first day of school. He probably had a dad who cared if some pervert tried to pull you into his car when you were walking home from a sleepover in the third grade. He didn't know what it was like to have to pretend it was your dad in the big orange city truck, following you to school just to make sure that you got there. Or, to hope that he really *was* happy to hear from you when you finally found his phone number, as a child, and he told you to call if you needed anything. Only to hear the, "I'm sorry, the number you have dialed has been disconnected" message, the next time you called. He probably didn't know that type of pain. Or, maybe he did.

The elevator smells musty. I am alone as the door opens to the second floor. I walk up to a desk that looks exactly like the one on the first floor. Do I have to do this again? It is a nurse this time, with a sweet, knowing smile. She doesn't need the same explanation. I say, "I am here to see my father."

I don't know why I said father. He was so unfather-like. I never called him that. It was way too official. I just keep going, afraid if I stop I might not be able to get it all out. "Mike Pritchard, his name is Mike Pritchard."

"Your dad is right behind you," she says.

I knew he was close. I could feel it. As I turned around, I expected I'd see the man I had always expected to see. The one he never was. He was supposed to be handsome, with dark hair and that wave in the front, as always. He was supposed to look like the pictures I looked at for hours as a child, trying to piece together who I wanted him to be. He looked a little like Elvis to me. He wore suits. He had cleats on the heels of his shoes, which made a funny sound when he walked. This man in the wheelchair, before me now, looked nothing like him. This man had white hair, and his eyes were a light baby blue. My dad had hazel eyes and was never in a wheelchair. He was six feet tall, and I had to reach up to hug him. Not anymore. This is my dad in the wheelchair. This shrunken old man, who is now shaking as he waits to hear what will happen next, is my dad.

The nurse says that he is almost blind now. I tell her he has been almost blind his whole life. I mean it in more ways than she knows. I feel compelled to redeem my sarcastic comment, however, by adding, "He got shot in the eye with a BB gun when he was a kid."

I step closer to him and drop into the chair next to the table where he has been eating his lunch. I feel my knees buckling as I sit down hard. "It's me, Dad," I said, "It's Dawn."

"Pooky Pritchard?" he says back to me, using the nickname that he has always used for me instead of my real name (no matter how old I get or how much time has passed). "My Pooky Pritchard?" he said. This time he is the one with tears streaming down his face.

"Yes, Dad, your Pooky Pritchard," I say, as I wipe his tears with the napkin in front of him.

I reach out for his hand and hold it as we sit in silence for what seems like an eternity. I have never seen my dad cry. What do I say now? I know I should say only nice things. He is old and ill, and I am a compassionate person, a grown-up. I know how to behave appropriately in this kind of situation. But, I have not come here to be nice. I have not come here to be mean. Without knowing it, I have come for answers, for both of us, for all of us.

Suddenly, the words just come out. The words I had said in my head for years but could never get them past the lump in my throat. "Dad, why do you keep leaving me?"

I braced myself for whatever would come at me. Some defensive comment or lie he had told himself like, "You didn't want to see me," or "The phone rings at both ends you know."

But he doesn't do that this time. He squeezes my hand and says, "Because I have been a selfish and bad man."

I say nothing. How can I disagree? We both know it is true. We both know that he needs to say it, and that I need to hear it. I sit in silence listening and wondering if he can still see well enough to see the stream of tears running down my cheeks. "Cheeks with dimples aren't supposed to have so many tears," he says. He can see me.

I still don't know why his eyes turned blue. Maybe they sometimes turn blue again, like when you're born. I wonder if that will happen to my eyes when I am old like he is.

"Pooky," he says, "You deserved a good dad, you all did, and your mom deserved a good husband. I wasn't that dad or husband. I hurt you all very much, and I am truly sorry. If I could take any of it back, I would. But, I can't fix it now. I could have, and I didn't. I am so sorry."

I tell him how much I missed having a dad. That I knew he worked for the city and drove a big orange truck. That I used to pretend, when I would see one, that it was him. I used to pretend he was following me to make sure I was all right or to see how much I had grown.

He said, "It should have been me in the big orange truck. It should have been me, and it wasn't. I am so sorry."

He was sorry. It was genuine. It was a gift.

I have to share it with the one who deserves it the most. I ask him if he wants to say anything to my mom, and he says, "Yes."

I wasn't sure how she would react, but I was dialing her number before I had thought it all through. "Mom," I said, "I'm sitting here with my dad, and he wants to say something to you. Do you want to talk to him?"

It would be her choice in the end. If she said no, I was going to hang up and he wouldn't get the chance. But I wanted her to hear, and I wanted her to forgive him—for herself—so she could finally heal the old hurt. She says she has already said everything she needs to say to him, but if there is something he needs to say, she will listen. I hold the phone up to his ear and say, "Dad, she is listening, you can talk now."

He says, "Donna, this is Mike." (As if she doesn't know.) "I want you to know how sorry I am for all of the pain that I caused you. You didn't deserve to be treated the way I treated you, and I am truly sorry."

There is silence on the other end. He looks at me as if to say, "I don't think she heard me. I don't think she is there."

But, I know that she is there. She is listening. She is just stunned because he has never said those words to her before. She composes herself long enough to say, "Thank you."

I take the phone back and say, "Mom is there anything else?"

"No, there is nothing else," she says.

He sighs as if a ton of bricks has been lifted from his chest. I think this was a good thing I have done for both of them, and for me.

After getting the information about his health, and why he is here in this health care facility instead of in his apartment, I tell him I have to leave soon. I tell him that I had been on my way to pick up Joy and my daughter, Molly, and that they are waiting for me. He lights up like a Christmas tree.

"Joy-Joy is here?" He always said my sister's name twice. "And M & M, too?" M & M was for Molly Marie.

I guess the nicknames helped him feel connected to us somehow, or gave the illusion of closeness. Maybe it was just because he was a kidder. "Yes, Dad, Joy-Joy and M&M are here in the city, and I will try to bring them to see you."

As I walk to the elevator, I think to myself that he knows how much it hurts now, and he is sorry. I hope my sister will be able to let him in one more time, as I have, for her. I also want my daughter to see her grandfather before the chance is gone. I am again on this road.

• • • • • •

Joy did agree to see him. I told her what hearing the things he had to say had done for me. I hoped that it would do the same for her. I was worried he might not be that person on the next visit. Would mistrust and inconsistency in our relationship exist until the end? That was the chance we were taking. If he were to act differently with her, at least this time we could blame it on his age and illness. I made no promises. We both knew that everything with him was a gamble. So, off we went—together.

Being so proud of my children, I was also anxious for him to see my daughter. I had seen him proud of my sons. Underneath it all, I wondered if he was proud of them because they were boys, in the same way he had been about his sons from his second family, my brothers.

I watch his tattered eyes, now a different color, admire my daughter's beauty, and he tells her so. I realize he said what he thinks is to be valued in girls, their beauty. He tells my daughter what a beautiful smile she has. He tells her to keep smiling. I think what he means is, "I hope you only have happiness in your life, and if other things come your way that you will find the ability to smile through it and be able to rise above any adversity that you may encounter."

I imagine he is thinking, "I wish that I could be there to protect you, as I wasn't there for your mother."

I can only hope. It is clear that he is proud of her, that he loves her, and that he wishes he could have been around, or would be around, to know her. We all knew that he would not. I watch my daughter's strength emerge as she graciously accepts the love and compliments from this grandfather she doesn't know. I believe now that she was given this opportunity as a gift to give her the strength she could use to get through the death of the grandfather she *did* know, her other grandfather, who would die a few years later.

Joy and Dad had a relationship that was different than mine with Dad. Their relationship had a past that was real, a past that she could remember, as she was the oldest daughter. I watch as she finds a way to touch on the good things of the past that they had together. They shared a love of music and singing. As we sit in this public place, the two of them sing "Somewhere Over the Rainbow." Their beautiful voices are clear in the song's message that dreams exist, that they can propel us, and that hope in tomorrow is always there.

That is the message I will remember. Love and forgiveness are the feelings I take with me, as I leave for what I know will be the last time I will ever see this man I call Papa.

The Last Visit

Joy

And so I went to see him one last time before leaving town. My annual summer trip to Minneapolis was about over. It is the end of July and time to return home to Tucson to start my work for the new school year. Dawn has already left for home. I am by myself. It is just me and him and decades of uneasiness.

He introduces me to the others at the table, in that proud way that fathers often do. I feel he really is proud. We talk. I sit with him while he tries to eat his dinner at a table full of old, frail men. These are people he doesn't know, but he is thrown together with by circumstance at this communal table. He tells me that when he gets out of this place, he is going to take all of the nurses and his new friends to a casino. He repeatedly says his mantra, "Somebody's gotta win. Why not me?"

After he finishes his dinner, he asks me to take him back down the hallway to his room. I wheel him back and help him into bed. His body is thin and fragile now. His bare feet are twisted, with yellowed nails. I cringe a bit to see him this way. This is not the body of the man I knew, who loved to pitch for the softball team. This is not the body of the man who played slots and blackjack at casinos through the night. But, this is what has become of him in his old age. He is living and eating with strangers and unable to care for himself.

As he is lying in bed, he says to me, “I know you think I loved the boys more, but I didn’t. I had five kids, and I loved you all the same.”

Although, we had never said that to him, never accused him of that, I know my sisters and I had thought it many times. We had thought that he chose his second family over us, gave them his love, because that family had two boys. His first family, my family, the one he abandoned, only had girls, three girls—my sisters and me.

It is a relief to hear him say it now. To say that what we had thought wasn’t true. Why couldn’t he have said it years before? Why couldn’t he have acknowledged what we meant to him before this? Why couldn’t he have told us what he loved about us? It would have meant so much to my sisters and me. Did he assume we just knew? Is that what he told himself? If that was it, then he assumed wrong. We didn’t know because he hadn’t told us.

I give him a hug and say I have to leave. We said our goodbyes.

As I am walking from his room to the elevator, he shouts out to me, “I love you, Joy-Joy.”

I shout back, “I love you too, Papa,” repeating it several

times until the elevator comes. I ride down and go out to the car, trying but failing to hold back the tears. I knew this would be the last time I'd see him.

The Legacy

Dawn

Dad died a few days after Joy returned to Tucson. Our sister, Bonnie, called to let us know the specifics. We now had to decide what we would do. Although, he had never dealt with the details of our lives, we would find over the next few weeks that we would be dealing with the details of his life, for the first time. We called our brothers in Nevada, and we all agreed it would be good to go to Minneapolis and be together.

We went through his apartment, which needed to be empty by the time we all got on our respective airplanes for home. Our brothers were doing the heavy lifting for him, as they had often done before. We all knew we would find nothing of monetary value. What we did find was that he had kept our grandma's rings. The rings that had caused the painful rift between him and Joy, were safe. She now wears them on Christmas Eve and other special occasions to honor the lasting legacy of our grandparents' love.

He had also kept many of the letters and pictures we had sent him over the years. He had not thrown them away in his many moves from Las Vegas to Minneapolis and back again. I came across a complete deck of cards, and at first I thought, of course, this is what was important to him. Then I realized that *his* deck was as complete as he could make it. In the end, he had not thrown us away.

As a group, we discussed what had to be done and what we could do. From that came the appropriate celebration for the man we knew.

More people came than I thought would. I was happy about that. Bonnie sang, as she had at both of our grandparents' (his parents) funeral services. I was awestruck, once again, at her ability to remain composed as she sang beautifully and clearly.

Joy spoke at the service and reminded us of his favorite saying about gambling, playing the lottery, and ultimately about his life. "Somebody's gotta win. Why not me?"

None of us lived in Minneapolis anymore. We were staying in hotels and driving rental cars, which created a dilemma. We had followed Dad's wishes for cremation. They gave him to us in an airline-approved plastic case that resembled a large video cassette case. He would be going home to Las Vegas (the place he loved the best, where he went to gamble and to be warm) with our brothers. None of us felt comfortable leaving him in a hotel room, or the trunk of a car, while we went where we went. Our brothers, whose role had in many ways always been picking up the pieces Dad would leave behind—this time it was literally, carried him everywhere we went in a back pack.

Our brothers said they wanted to keep a promise they had made to Dad to take him to dinner at Murray's, his favorite piano bar/restaurant in downtown Minneapolis. Dad and Murray's went way back. He sang at their piano bar in his younger days and always liked coming back. So, here he was again, this time with all five of his children, something which had rarely occurred during his lifetime.

The time we spent together as sisters and brothers had immeasurable healing qualities for me. We laughed loud and hard, sometimes until we cried. We reminisced about the reality of our dad's life. We forgave him and loved him, as a group. He had never been a generous gift-giver. But I realized as I looked across the table at my wonderful siblings, he had given us the best gift that he could have given.

He had given us each other.

Birthday Tribute

Bonnie

FUN

• From playing broomball & ice skating on the frozen Minnesota rinks, to teaching your nieces to boogie board in the California surf,

• From acting as the Wicked Witch in your college production of "The Wizard of Oz," to performing as the Dove Lady in the Easter Pageant at your church.

• From dressing up in creative costumes (a tube of toothpaste), to your eagerness to participate in throwing whipped cream pies in each other's faces,

you remind us how important it is to feel like we are kids again, and inspire us to continue to have fun at any age.

MUSIC

• From singing along with the Lawrence Welk TV show as a kid,

• to working as a music consultant for the Welk Group and Pat Boone,

• From making up your own lyrics to classic Christmas songs, to your present day unwavering ability to sing in the most awe-inspiring moments,

• From listening to great singers and rock & roll bands on LP's & 45's, to producing compilation CD's preserving artistry for the future,

you remind us of the power of music, and inspire us with your beautiful voice.

PETS

• From rescuing a mouse from a cat when you were playing as a kid in the neighborhood, to rescuing your kittens Gracie & Bella from the shelter,

• From growing up in a house in Minneapolis filled with dogs, cats, birds, hamsters and a duck, to traveling across the country with your cat Misha,

• From helping to teach our dog Trixie to say "herro" (hello), to your search and rescue of Misha after the earthquake in L.A.,

you remind us that pets are part of our family, and inspire us with the special bond you share with your pets.

FAITH

• From the baby looking up at her mom with surprise in her blue eyes as if to say "where am I?", to the confident accomplished woman who still loves surprises,

• From walking to Sunday School in the Minnesota snow, to your devotion to your California and Virginia churches,

• From earning your degrees (Early Childhood/Community Education), to your commitment in the fight against human trafficking,

you remind us of the power of prayer, and inspire others in the strength of faith.

• • • • • •

I've thought about how I would finish my story. Obviously, I'm still here, and my story is not over. At this moment, I'm thinking about you, the reader of these stories, and I'm wondering if you might have walked a path similar to mine or to that of my sister, Joy. I wonder if you have had some of the same feelings or wishes along your journey.

My hope is if there is a person in your life to whom you have wanted to say something—something that is good about who that person is, or what he or she means to you—you will tell that person now. Don't wait, or assume, or tell someone else and hope your message gets to the person. Swallow your pride, or that lump in your throat, and tell him or her. Believe me, this person wants to hear it and might even have been waiting to hear it.

Then, continue on with the next person, and then the next.

How do I complete my story that continues? There is still so much that can be said. I'm grateful for another day and another year to hold my family near. We'll throw our cards in the air and wait with eager eyes to see where they fall. We'll continue to grow through communication, commitment, love and by giving tribute to the best in each of us.

Gifts from Others and the Gifts We Give Ourselves

Joy

Getting through the difficult parts of life and moving on is not an easy thing to do. There have been hard times. I did lose some things, but I found even more. I was determined that I would not be defined by the abandonment of a father, the end of a marriage, or a disease. And, although I am single, I am not alone.

My sisters and my mom offered me their strength when I could not use my own. As the oldest sibling, I had always felt it was my role to set the example for my sisters. It was my responsibility to watch out for them on the slide or in the swimming pool, to hold their hands as we walked down the steps or crossed the street. When I needed their strength, they offered it, and I accepted. I relied on it to get me through.

My niece Molly, always wise beyond her years, offered me her unconditional love. She calls me her "Joie," but in reality *joie* is what she brings to me. From the birth of her first child over 30 years ago, Dawn has generously included me in the raising of her children. I have loved and cared for them as my own. I cherish this most precious gift.

• • • • • •

Shortly after that trip to Mexico in the 1970s, Merry gave me a gift of a piece of stained glass. The scene it depicts is of a beach, complete with the bluest water, fan shaped shells, white seagulls, a big yellow sun, and a quote from *Emerson* which says, "A friend may well be the masterpiece of nature." Merry was the quintessential friend, a masterpiece of nature. Her presence in my life, so long ago, continues to inspire me.

I made new commitments. I made a commitment to myself that I would spend a part of every summer in my hometown of Minneapolis, the beautiful city of lakes. I would reach out and share real time with my Minneapolis friends, not just an occasional holiday card or phone call. This would be a time for us to talk, to be together, to share experiences, as we did in our earlier years when hanging out with your friends *was* your first priority. We would go to Lake Nokomis and walk from little beach to big beach and then back again. I would come back when my favorite band had a gig, and I'd be there in the audience as I'd been so many times as a teenager. We'd have picnics at Minnehaha Falls. And, we would make time to sit and talk about where we came from, where we were heading, and the things on our minds.

We see the sparkle of where we came from in each other's

eyes.

Phill and I have been friends since we were teenagers. We first met in the summer of 1969, at the big three-day Mid-West Rock Festival being held in Wisconsin. I met Phill as we listened to Jeff Beck, Jethro Tull, Joe Cocker, Buffy Saint Marie, Led Zeppelin, and Blind Faith. We ended up riding back to Minneapolis in the same car. Phill became like a brother to me. He was my first roommate. He was the first vegetarian I knew. Later that year, I would also become a vegetarian—for life.

The other day I was walking through a Tucson grocery store, and I heard an announcement to "visit our meat department and pick up some fresh chicken." I thought to myself, if Phill were here, he and I would crack up laughing about that statement. We would question what's "fresh" about dead chicken.

We have been connected through so many of life's passages. I appreciate his remarkable wit and wisdom, his integrity, his loyalty, and his astute political insights.

I am grateful to my Minneapolis family of friends for the gift of life-long friendships.

"A friend is someone who knows the song in your heart, and can sing it back to you when you have forgotten the words." *Anonymous.*

• • • • • •

Music is my enduring passion. I am both a participant and a listener. I remember sitting up in my room in the 1960s, with my transistor radio to my ear, listening to their songs. I remember rushing out to take the bus to the record store to buy their first album. I remember taking a trip downtown to see their first movie. But most of all, I remember how I loved (and still do) their music. They were the Beatles.

My junior high friend and I couldn't wait to see each other in homeroom the morning after their first appearance on the Ed Sullivan Show. We gushed about it endlessly. The whole school was buzzing about them. So, in the spring of 1965, when they announced their U.S. stadium concert tour and Minneapolis was on the list, we knew we would find a way to go. We just had to.

Tickets were only being sold through mail order. To get a ticket, you had to send in a check or a money order along with a self-addressed envelope. As a 13-year-old, of course, I didn't have a checking account. So, I walked up to our corner grocery store and bought a money order for the ticket price. The ticket cost a grand total of $4.50. I checked the mail every day waiting anxiously for my self-addressed envelope to be returned. When I finally received it, there was a minor problem. I hadn't known that the seating in the baseball stadium would be assigned seats. My Beatle-buddy and I had sent for our tickets separately, so we would not be sitting together.

The night of the concert finally came on August 21, 1965. My friend's mom drove us to Metropolitan Stadium, and there in the parking lot we made plans for a place to rendezvous after the concert. Then, I went off to find my seat. At first I was a little scared being in such a big place, with such a big crowd, by myself. But, eventually, it didn't matter. Once the music started I wasn't alone—I was with the Beatles. They played a dozen songs that night, including "Twist and Shout" and "A

Hard Day's Night." I hung on every word, every note, their every movement, and every shake of their heads. After the last song, as they were running from their stage to the dugout, I just know Paul looked up at me and waved. Beatles 4-Ever. That was my first concert.

The old stadium was torn down a few years ago to make way for the Mall of America. When I'm in Minneapolis, I always make time for some shopping at the mega-mall. But retail therapy aside, when I first walk in I take a moment to remember this is the place where I was privileged to see and hear the Beatles. It is hallowed ground.

It was Christmas time in 1999, when I finished cancer treatment, and Bonnie came to spend the holidays with us in Tucson. We were in the car driving over to Dawn's house when Bonnie began singing Christmas carols. The car-singer in me automatically joined in on harmony. I realized as I was singing that I had not sung for the six months since cancer had entered my world. That was so unlike me—I am someone who usually sings every day. I hadn't felt like myself for many months. But, as soon as we finished the first carol, I began to feel a little bit better, more like myself. At that moment, I experienced the powerful healing effects that singing has for me.

I made a commitment to myself that I would bring more music into my life. I wanted to sing again. I needed to sing again. But, I wanted to sing better than I ever had before. I wanted my voice to soar.

I needed a voice coach who could help me develop my neglected instrument. I met Eric at a house concert that he was hosting for a touring musician. When I heard him sing and play his music, I felt a deep connection. I knew I could entrust my instrument to his care. He understands that the voice, like any instrument, needs technique and practice in order to improve. He has the critical ear that I need to hear every nuance in my voice. He corrects me when it's wrong, praises me when it's right, and pushes me to do better. He helps me to express the lyrics, by digging deep and trying to give every ounce of meaning to a song. That was sometimes hard to do for a girl raised in the stoicism of Scandinavian traditions. But he found ways. We have found ways together.

In his song titled "True Friends" from his *Hero in the Dark* CD, Eric sings, "True friends, fall right out of the blue. True friends, sneak right up on you. When you least expect a miracle, and you can not find your shoes, and every hall's a dark one, somehow they find you." (Reprinted by permission from Eric Hansen, Hansen Oil Well—ASCAP).

I am so grateful to my true friend, Eric, for his beautiful music, his generosity in sharing his musical talents and abilities with me, for helping me to develop my own, and now on occasion allowing me to sing and perform with him.

I know I can not get through without the gift of music.

• • • • • •

And, I kept my promise to myself. I have made it back to my favorite place by the ocean. I walk along the beach of golden sand and feel at peace. I see the sunlight sparkle off of the blue water, hear the roar of the waves, and smell the sea breeze. And,

I'm bringing people with me!

It started as a "school's out for summer trip" for my niece Molly and me. Then my sisters, Dawn and Bonnie, and my great-niece, Juliet, began to join in, and it became a "girl's trip." On occasion, my brother-in-law, Michael, and my nephews, Jesse and Bryan, join in on what has now become an annual trip.

Some of the writing of this book has occurred at this special place.

We have listened to our hearts and told our stories. And, as Dawn and I sit on the beach watching Molly and Juliet playing in the surf and running alongside the ocean's shore scooping up sand dollars and shells in their little plastic buckets, my heart is full with the riches of my life.

Birthday Tributes

Joy's Birthday Tribute 2

Another year, what can we add?

Let's think of all of the fun we've had.

We've gone home to The Cities. We've been to The Del.

We've laughed, we've cried, we've worked like hell.

But through it all, we've been together.

We've mastered some, enjoyed the weather.

What can we add to what still holds true?

Those things we feel are what make you—you.

There are things that are left to say.

We are grateful for another year, in which to hold our Joy so dear.

More time to celebrate who you are, a hand to hold, a budding star.

So when we can, we'll put our feet in the sand.

We'll throw our cards in the air and see where they land.

We will be grateful for each week, month and day.

And that we have our Joy with us along to play.

Dawn's Birthday Tribute 2

♥

For our celebration this year of what makes you—you,
What can we add to what still holds true?
We do have more we want to say,
This comes from our hearts to yours for your Birthday!
We admire and appreciate you for:
your kindness, your loyalty,
being a great mom and friend,
your ability to persevere when times are difficult,
not giving up, always following through,
your hard work and many accomplishments.
We turn to you for:
advice, comfort, and to lift us up,
your wisdom, your level-headedness,
answers and help with life,
and friendship.
You make a difference to us and the world because:
you are always there for us,
you have our backs,
you do things to make everyone happy,
and you have a heart as pure as gold.
You have taught us:
compassion, patience and understanding,
how to listen, about the world,
about the importance of keeping commitments,
to follow the dreams in our hearts,
and to always reach for the stars.

Part Three

~

How to Write a Tribute

The Purpose:

To those you love, tell them why, tell them now

A Birthday Tribute is a way to honor and celebrate those special people in your life for whom a greeting card just doesn't say enough. When you find yourself standing in the card aisle reading several of them, and none of them seems right, you need more than a card. You need a Birthday Tribute.

The simple purpose of the Tribute is to tell a person what he or she means to you. It is a tool to help express what, unfortunately, oftentimes goes unsaid. The gift of a Tribute enhances a birthday. It adds more meaning to the event, making the birthday a very memorable celebration.

This is a gift that will last. It never needs returning. It doesn't go out of style. It always fits. It doesn't cost money. To the recipient, it will be priceless.

The Process:

You can do this

The process begins with deciding who will be the Tribute's author. You, the reader of this book, may (or may not) be the best person to serve as the author of the Tribute. In our experience, the best author is the person who is the closest to the recipient. If that is not you, then you may want to share this book with that person, or assist them in writing the Tribute. The author will reach out to the participants, gathering their thoughts and memories for inspiration. Then, the author decides on the form and writes the Tribute.

Although the Tribute needs an author, it should not be written solely from one person's perspective. In the process of creating a Tribute, the author asks those people closest to the recipient to reflect on the positive attributes of the recipient. As Dawn did when writing the first Tribute to Joy, you can begin by asking the simple question, "What do you love about *this person*?" All ages can participate and, in fact, will have unique perspectives to contribute. The author then uses these different perspectives to create a multi-dimensional Tribute.

Sometimes, participants tend to focus on themselves instead of on the recipient. We have found that using prompts can be helpful in getting the participant to focus on the recipient.

The author asks the participants to focus on the positive attributes of the recipient and to bring those to the surface (letting go of the negative). The following questions are prompts we have found to be useful (insert the name of your recipient in place of *this person)*:

1. What do you like best about *this person*?
2. What do you admire and appreciate about *this person*?
3. How does *this person* make a difference to you?
4. How does *this person* make a difference to our family?
5. How does *this person* make a difference to the world?
6. What has *this person* taught you?
7. What special memories do you have of *this person*?

We have also found that photos can be an aid in helping jog the memories of the participants. This is a perfect time to get out those photos you've collected through the years and enjoy them. What are you waiting for?

You may find some people are reluctant to participate. We have found that sometimes this is because the person may feel that what he or she has to say is not important, or it is not good enough. Or, the person may assume that the recipient already knows how he or she feels. It could be because the person feels words are not enough to express what is truly in his or her heart.

Whatever the reason, these barriers may become excuses for not participating. We have found that even the simplest expression, when heartfelt, is valuable to the recipient.

If you encounter a reluctance to participate, it can become an opportunity to have a discussion with the participant about the importance of acknowledging what we mean to each other. This part of the Tribute process can be valuable for the participant's own personal growth. It may help the reluctant participant open up and begin to develop a new way to express him or herself.

Focusing on the positive can help all of the participants develop better ways to communicate. This is a chance to let go of the negative communication patterns that people occasionally fall into. Sometimes our communication patterns tend to be very critical. We may complain about the faults and weaknesses we see in each other. But, how often do we focus on the positive? What could happen if we changed this communication pattern? Use this Tribute process as an opportunity to begin this change. Take a look at this person from a positive point of view, and focus on his or her best qualities.

The form of your written Tribute can be done in any organizational style you choose. We have used several different forms, which are included in Parts One and Two of this book. The easiest form is simply to use the headings from your prompts (for examples, see the Tributes to Jesse, Molly, and Dawn's Tribute 2).

You might also use a form that plays off of the recipient's name or meaningful words (for examples, see the Tributes to Dawn, Mom, Juliet, and Bonnie). You could also create a

Tribute in the form of a story (for examples, see the Tributes to Joy, Michael, Bryan, and Joy's Tribute 2).

The words of a Tribute should not be measured by their grammatical perfection. The Tribute's value is in its personal heartfelt messages. Like the lyrics of a song or the lines of a poem, a Tribute may not always be written in perfect English. Write the Tribute in a style that works best for your family of participants. Remember, as the author, you are gathering contributions from others. Their messages should come through in their own words.

Take a special moment during the recipient's birthday party to gather together, and then read the Tribute aloud. This is a wonderful opportunity for all to be present and honor the recipient. Most of all, love will be present in that moment.

The Result

Illuminate the Positive

The process of creating a Tribute can begin to open the channels of communication and strengthen the connections among the family of participants. As they dig deep to share their thoughts about the recipient, the participants can create a loving and warm-hearted sense of community.

In writing the Tribute, the author shines a light on the positive attributes of the recipient. By illuminating the positive, we can begin to change the ways in which we communicate. The Tribute is a way to "start the conversation." It celebrates the good.

Tell people what they mean to you. Don't just assume they know. Don't wait.

Honor the best in a person. Reflect it back to them. They will see it in themselves.

Epilogue—The Letter in the Book

Joy

Today is my birthday. Along with the feeling that it is a privilege to have another birthday, comes the sometimes difficult realization of the ageing process. As many of us do, I tell myself, "But, hey it's only a number!"

Dawn and I started the Birthday Tributes for my birthday one year ago today. We've now been through a full year's cycle of Birthday Tributes for everyone in our family. This morning, I'm thinking about the past year and the many unexpected things (some of them total surprises) that have occurred during the process of writing the actual Birthday Tributes, and during the writing of this book. Here is one that happened to me.

One Saturday morning, I wrote the story of my move to Tucson. That story would become the Chapter "From Cold to Hot." I was very excited to have Dawn read it, so I grabbed the rough draft and brought it over to her house. I told her it was a draft, and I still needed to finalize it. Part of that finalization included verifying the proper spelling of the indigenous peoples in Oaxaca, Mexico. I would do that when I went back home. I thought I might still have a book that I had picked up during my Mexico trip with Merry those many years ago. The authentic spellings should be in that book. I hoped I hadn't recycled the book the previous summer when I had gone through a major purge of household stuff. Getting rid of extraneous stuff is such a cleansing, freeing feeling for me. It lightens my load. But, the danger is in getting rid of something you might still need sometime. Fortunately, I hadn't done that. The book was still there in my bookcase.

As my thumb fluttered through the pages, I found the letter. It was tucked deep between the pages of the book. A book I now realize I must not have even opened for 30 years or so. I had written and mailed this letter from Minneapolis in April 1975. It was sent to a guy I had met in Tucson in March. We were in love, and I was back in Minneapolis packing and making plans to move to live with him in Tucson. The letter was folded inside its original (opened) envelope and postmarked April 22, 1975. The words were full of the promise of young love. It was overflowing with my excitement at the possibilities for our future together. It was written from the heart of the twenty-something me.

It was, of course, a pre-email and pre-cell phone world. We didn't have money for what was in the 1970s expensive long distance telephone calls. So, we wrote letters. My Tucson Guy must have saved the letter until I arrived in Tucson. Then, one of us had tucked it in this book, maybe for safekeeping, or maybe it was just being used as a bookmark. Whatever the reason, here it was now, and it was a gift. And, what a gift! I was able to go back in time for a moment and experience how I felt, and what was in the heart of the twenty-something me.

I excitedly called Dawn and said, "You aren't going to believe what I found!" She was amazed and said, "What ever happened to him?" I didn't know the answer to that question. By the late 1970s, that love had burned itself out. We had both closed the door and moved on. Some doors are better left closed. But finding an old friend can also be like finding buried treasure. Now I was curious to see if I could find him, so I used modern technology and logged on to my facebook account. Within about 30 seconds, I thought I'd found him.

Without hesitation, I emailed him, simply saying, "Hello—are you the person I used to know in Tucson, Arizona?" And within a few days I received this reply. "Aloha Joy—Well, yes and no is the answer to your question. First of all, the Joy I knew in Tucson was a ravishing brunette, while you are a beautiful blonde :-) Also, the person you knew was very young, and I'm much older and wiser now :-)"

My Tucson Guy now lives happily in California. We have had a great time filling each other in on the paths our lives have traveled over the past three decades. I am grateful for our reconnection as long lost friends—now found.

There is no logical reason that the letter should have survived all of these years. I've moved several times and cleaned out books many times over the years. But there it was, tucked deep inside the pages and waiting for me to find it at the perfect time.

Acknowledgments and Appreciation

To our publisher, Lin Conklin: for her steadfast integrity and her belief in authors.

To Bryan Burruel: for his artistry in creating our cover artwork and illustration.

To Molly Burruel: for her 21st century punctuation skills and teaching us to use the em dash.

Joy

To my Minneapolis friends—Phill, Mary, Nancy, Kerry, Marilyn, Jerry, Denny, Bonnie, and Tom: Thanks for your life-long friendships, welcoming me back every summer (and for storing my stuff).

To my Tucson friends and colleagues—Eric, Joni, Richard, Rita, Julianna, Eleanor, Dave, Mary Z., Julie, Linda, Laurie, Francisca, Phil (formerly of Tucson), Katie, and Blue Raven

Gallery: Thanks for your friendships, birthday celebrations, support, and encouragement.

To my family—Mom, Bonnie, Molly, Juliet, Michael, Jesse, and Bryan: Thanks for everything but most of all for your love and inspiration.

To my sister—Dawn: Thanks for your collaboration on this book and throughout life. For always being there for me, no matter what, with your underlying, unconditional love. For being the person I can always count on to be my sounding board.

Dawn

Thank you to:

My sister, Joy: for laying many beautiful paths and inviting me to travel them with her.

My husband, Michael: for always believing in me and telling me so, out loud. For showing me what a dad can be and giving me a reason to celebrate Father's Day. For teaching me (what you learned from the beautiful love that your parents shared) a marriage can last if it contains both love and commitment.

My son, Jesse, my first born: for being my inspiration to always at least consider the alternative.

My son, Bryan: for being my own personal Batman.

My daughter, Molly: If you weren't my daughter, you would still be one of my favorite people to hang out with.

My mother, Donna; my sister, Bonnie; and my granddaughter, Juliet: for loving me no matter what.

My BFF's Kim and Dawn M.: for sharing life's journeys, no matter how busy we all are or how much time has passed, for showing me time can stand still when we are together, and for putting your lives on hold when I come home to Minneapolis.

My friend, Frank Williams of Frank Williams Design: for sharing your endless encouragement.

My friend, Sandra Morse: for your friendship, which enhances my life, and your being, which enhances the world. For teaching me I could change my own internal conversation and the ways in which I communicate with others.

My mentor, Pamela McNair Wingate: for seeing potential in me and giving me incredible opportunities for personal and professional growth. For your inspiration in striving to live, love, and work each day to one's fullest potential. For telling me I could write and that what I wrote would be read.

CPSIA information can be obtained at www.ICGtesting.com
Printed in the USA
BVOW020732131011

273490BV00001B/2/P

9 781935 354628